Love
EXPRESSIONS

ARPress LLC
45 Dan Road Suite 5
Canton MA 02021
Hotline: 1(888) 821-0229
Fax: 1(508) 545-7580

Ordering Information:
Quantity sales. Special discounts are available on quantity purchases by corporations, associations, and others. For details, contact the publisher at the address above.

Printed in the United States of America.

ISBN-13: Softcover   979-8-89330-683-5
          eBook   979-8-89330-682-8

Library of Congress Control Number: 2024902576

Love
EXPRESSIONS

OWENAZEE G. IMAFIDON

ARPress
ILLUMINATING IDEAS
EMPOWERING VOICES

My Shining Star

Only you are my knight and armor

You are my bright morning star and a shield from the troubles of life

Oh baby I want to be right here were you are till our dying days

You are the love of my life and without you my life will be lonely

The thought of not seeing you troubles the peace in my heart

only you complete me and you have become a garment of healing
    to my soul

LISTEN TO YOUR HEART

Listen to your heart and hear it speak

With absolute obedience to your heart you will go places

Loneliness will never be your portion be at peace when I call for you

Your central command lies in your heart and it will reveal to you
your dreams

Be determined so your plan can be achieved because it will be difficult if you have no heart to direct your path there.

Your heart is full of love and it is purely ready for acceptance

DESERT RAIN

She has the force of a storm that's why your boldness is incomparable to no one

You are the backbone of this family, and a tree to lean on

Please swallow your pride and let's be together so we can achieve
God's master plan for us

Humility should be your peace of mind

You are the desert rain that came to wipe out my life struggles

We all need somebody to lean on so God sent you to be my minis-
tering angel

With your love my struggles were evaporated at once

So I humbly say thanks from the bottom of my heart.

PEACE AND LOVE

Picture peace and love together

Oasis is their result so lets get ready to achieve

Neither peace nor love will deny your entrance because you have the antidote they need

Your movement is undetectable because you are an energetic human being

Mobility is your companion that's why God gave you those sexy legs

Your beauty from the crown of your head to the sole of your feet is in a class of its own

You are that lady a man will repent from his sick ways to have.

Your presence has changed my sleepless night to a peaceful one.

Soul-Mate

For this reason a man shall leave his mother and father to cleave
    unto his soul mate

That is who you are we were destined to be together

So God made you from the mari-clay to be my other half

You are a match made from heaven

I'm glad you are the flesh of my flesh

Our ministry on earth is forever and time cannot deny us

My heart is your home where you will always find rest

This dress is perfect for you and it completes you

I promise to love and respect you.

My Hero

You are the one I love because you are my hero

You are the one I love because I want you to always be mine

I don't care what your past entails because your heart is what I'm
aiming for to

receive peace and absolute acceptance

You are my hero and a woman to be a queen to this king

You are the one I love please be my hero and I will stand by you
forever

You are my hero because you took my breath away

You are my hero because you are full of life and laughter

You are my hero because I know you will die for me even if I didn't
ask you to.

ME TO YOU

From me to you is who you deserve

To love and cherish you never to suffer

In my heart you are number one and always will be

Even if I can't have you is all good

They say blood is thicker than water

But I say love is stronger than hate.

So you can love me or hate me

I will still stand with you

Hopefully my essence will touch you because

I'm nothing you've never experienced only better that is all

Of-course it can be tasteful sweeter than our phone conversations

So what is love if there is no giving and appreciation.

I know your heart is as peaceful as the sand by the seashore

So let's come together please remember the romance

the dinner in bed how I've cooked for you

This love will never die

I'll hold it for you until you return into my heart.

You deserve this heart

You deserve his heart because his love for you is stronger than life

When he is one he is still but a peek at your smile his heart giggles

So you deserve this heart that you will be cherished and never to suffer

His heart is full of warmth for you though his body does not know you but his spirit loves you,

before he met you God made you his bride in the spirit relm.

You deserve his heart because he can feel your heart singing at church when you joined the choir.

Ms. Mercy Egharevba is her name, an intelligent queen whom this king has fallen for.

There are things he wants to say but fear grips him until now because he has disregarded fear for love even if there is no interest in him from her heart.

He still loves you. His heart is in love with that lady who is his future bride.

COME ON LOVE

Come on love your complexion is prettier than ever

Come on love you are my duplicate if you see me in your dream
tonight

Come on love you are always positive even when things are not right
you remain closer to me

Come on love in you I find no discouragement that's why you are
the love of my life.

Come on love I thank God he brought you into my life just as he
did for Isaac through his father Jacob check Genesis for revela-
tions and interpretation

Come on love if love is a game then count me out because this is real
I can't help it

Come on love what I feel for you is stronger than words

Come on love that's why I have to let it out because my heart can't
contain it.

Come on love is you and I forever

Come on love you are always looking fly you glow more than diamonds

Come on love you are the queen of my life and without you I'm empty

Come on love because of you I will give up my bad habits even drinking

Come on love make your request known and I will grant it

Come on love even more you will never lack it's a promise

Come on love this is what it is a proposal please accept me

More of you

More of you is what I need

Peace and joy can't succeed without you

Your presence is like a sweet aroma

The most beautiful of all women

That's why I love you

Let me kiss you with the kisses of my mouth

My breath is sweeter than honey and sugar combine

Taste it and it will melt you.

Even yet sweeter than orgasm because it's anointed with love

Life without you is uncertain more of you is what I need

You are my queen never to be deserted

the future mother of my children

More of you is what I need

The source of my strength without you getting up daily is a joke

You are the motivation of my life.

You are the most incredible person because you complete me

You deserve this heart

You deserve his heart because his love for you is stronger than life

When he is one he is still but a peak at your smile his heart giggles

So you deserve this heart that you will be cherished and never to suffer

His heart is full of warmth for you though his body does not know you but his spirit loves you,

before he met you God made you his bride in the spirit relm.

You deserve his heart because he can feel your heart singing at church when you joined the choir.

Ms. Mercy Egharevba is her name, an intelligent queen whom this king has fallen for.

There are things he wants to say but fear grips him until now because he has disregarded fear for love even if there is no interest in him from her heart.

He still loves you. His heart is in love with that lady who is his future bride.

Come on love

Come on love your complexion is prettier than ever

Come on love you are my duplicate if you see me in your dream
tonight

Come on love you are always positive even when things are not right
you remain closer to me.

Come on love in you I find no discouragement that's why you are
the love of my life.

Come on love I thank God he brought you into my life just as he
did for Isaac through his father Jacob check Genesis for revela-
tions and interpretation

Come on love if love is a game then count me out because this is
real I can't help it

Come on love what I feel for you is stronger than words

Come on love that's why I have to let it out because my heart can't
contain it.

Come on love is you and I forever

Come on love you are always looking fly you glow more than diamonds

Come on love you are the queen of my life and without you I'm empty

Come on love because of you I will give up my bad habits even drinking

Come on love make your request known and I will grant it

Come on love even more you will never lack it's a promise

Come on love this is what it is a proposal please accept me

I DON'T WANT TO LEAVE YOU

Not tonight I just want to hold you so we can conversate

Sex is not an item in this ordeal because what I feel for you is much
more than that

An elegant queen is who you are to me and you will never be a slave

so let me hold you and show you what is like to be hailed and treated
as such.

The most beautiful afro centric queen is who you are to me

You are the formula in my heart, that's why love is uniting us

I prayed for you even before I spoke to you

My aim for you is to be the flesh of my flesh and the bone of my
bone,

Tonight I just want to hold you because romance is what we need
after the conversations

I can be your undivided attention and whenever you need me I
promise to be there for you

I don't want to leave you so let me hold you and this is not a game
maybe we can be one forever.

Come on love so we can be tighter together like before never to be separated forever.

Come on love jealous ones still envy so I want you in my arms in our own relm

Private life is sweeter than public come on love just you and I together.

A real soldier at heart and the most talented is who you are

you are never to be abused and deserted

You are the kind that has the healing antidote I have been searching for

Your presence is calming and my heart has stopped wondering because my wife is here.

Please be mine,

Ms. Simone

She so quiet as ever your presence is more silent than stealth

your hair smell so nice it must be the head and shoulder shampoo

Your breath glides by my face and it smell like that fragrance you
always use

Come on girl you know your are sassy and lovely always compare
to no other

So what's your secret and motivation is it me because if it is then
I'm yours

Your skin is so beautiful I can feel it from afar, it must be that cocoa
butter

The way you speak is incomparable to all other women I have
known.

I'm yours for the taken so come and lets be together.

This is more than a fantasy because time waits for no one but for
you I will delay.

The thought of you leaving is scary it feels as if my future is bleek
without you

I know you feel the same because I'm in your wavelength so don't
switch the channel

An average woman just what I was looking for thank God I finally
found you.

The mother of all mothers is your future

I can see it happening from afar through an eagle's eye this it's a
prophecy

This relm is ours and never to be taken from us so let focus

If you stand with me we can make it

She said to love and to beheld forever

To be her companion and never to leave her

My heart dropped and I said then I'm yours because you are the one
I have been waiting for.

OASIS

Her name was Jackie

She was my oasis

She had cat eyes

so pretty anxiety shooked me

When I opened my mouth to speak I became speechless

She smiled at me and said hello young man what's your name?

I gasped for breath for she was a most beautiful creature my eyes has
ever upheld

Um my name is Darius Wisdom I said

She looked at me and smile again this time her teeth was whiter than
snow.

A few minutes later I remember grandma's spirit echoing in my ears
son do what you do best just talk to her.

I gather myself and I stepped up to her

Ms Jackie welcome to oasis this relm is mine please step in.

I like you so lets be together but first we must conversate

So I can be your minister for the time being until you know the real me.

So I asked her what was her destination

She said oasis so I said I'm your angel and I came just for you

I want to make you mine and never to let you go

Seeing you made my system numb and almost dumb

If you can make a wish what would it be?

ENROUTE TO LOVE

What is love if giving is not involved

What is love if we cannot respect one another

What is love if all we do is bicker with one another

What is love if hatred is the result

Love can be stronger than what you feel if we put feelings aside

Because love is caring and feelings

Love is an equation every failing relationship should desire

Love is when you submit to one another in respect of God's will

Love is when you can turn back around and bless those you resented
for all your hurts

Love is a place where two go to rest and gather themselves together

Love is a place that is more peaceful than oasis even quieter than the
streams of water

Love is a place stronger than the tree of life planted by the river's of
water

It is like a rose when it is enroute to budding

More silent than the sound of peace

It does not disapprove regardless of conditions

Most importantly love is unconditional if you allow it to grow in the
right direction

Love in the end is a gift that can overcome all things

A gift that is our master key to happiness

Beautiful Mind

What a beautiful gift from God

you are to be cherished never to be abandon, cared for and nurtured.

Your presence is full of essence and time is your key to perfection

Understanding is your servant to success and knowledge will serve
you as you respect him most especially wisdom will always guide
you so long you are humble before God and man.

Believe me this same blessing was pronounced on Samuel and Christ.

Remember one thing action taken appropriately is better than
unused knowledge

Though they say knowledge is power.

Please check to see so you can aim right and higher because what
you don't experience cannot strengthen your faith and without
faith life is meaningless.

I know you are capable because your empowerment is from the most
high King.

So you are an angel I love your smile

keep smiling I know you are going to be a successful woman.

Keep your head up and make sure you respect your dad no matter
what.

BEAUTY

What is beauty if it cannot be unveiled

Beauty should be displayed purely from a sweet and tender heart

so it can glow like the sun

Essence is the aim of beauty

if the right applications are used in the process to showcase it

Anticipation should not be a distraction to beauty even if the wait
seem forever

Unruly heart cannot display your beauty because your virtues lies
in your heart

Togetherness will always exemplify beauty and rescue it from
suffering

Your aim is to love and respect beauty while it stands

A wonderful thing to be cherished like a man's feelings when he is
fallen for a woman

It does not complain about the unnecessary nor does it grumbles
rarely

Love is just a connection that finally meets its right partner like tying two strings together.

Love is unbreakable like the ying and the yang symbol

Love Cares deeply.

Echoes of love

I could not smell hate when I kissed you

You have an afro sensual lips destined for tenderness

I will remember what you went through just to be by my side

Through it all you stayed

The illness almost took me but your effectual prayer and steadfast-
ness Kept me

You are the intercessor of my life what a wonderful custodian

Because you are a gift from God I will cherish you forever

Reward will be your wealth and wisdom will be your clothing

You are a sweet heart to be remembered and never to be forgotten
Your ministry in my life is full of grace and love

Favor will be your blouse and understanding will be your blanket

I will never leave you nor hurt you

I will always give you the keys to my heart whenever you need it
Love always from your king.

THE QUEEN IN MY LIFE

She's irresistibly unbelievable

You glow brighter than sun shine

If loving you is wrong then I'm all for it

Your presence and warmth I cannot describe

It is more alive than my heartbeat

You are a place calmer than the formula of God in my heart

You are my queen and I cannot deny your reception now

Remember when we first met I still feel the same way

You fed me when I was hungry and you took my heart hostage

When I was sick you stayed by my bedside until I was released

You are a gift from above destined for greatness

I promise I will support your dreams like you supported mine

Love should be our aim

Your prayers cannot be forgotten

You are a blessed soul created just for me

I thank God you complete me

Heartfelt Breath

HER EYES

Her eyes are brighter than angel eyes

Radiating from here to there

You are a woman of status,

that's why you are in a class of your own

You are an intellectual icon

Sent to earth by God, you are in Genesis

With those eyes unnoticing you is impossible

Loving you is a pleasure never to be forgotten

Your presence clothe me at night especially during those lonely nights in the field

As a marine in the wilderness thoughts of coming home to see you encouraged me

Oppressing the enemies of my country reminded me of times spent playing chess

BLACK OR WHITE

What can I say is love black or white

Is it full of grace

Can forgiveness be the answer love needs

Should desperation be an uncle to love

Is love a requirement of life

When a man rape a woman is that love or lust

Can an angry soul ever feel loved

Should Love be reduced

What does love has to say

Will black ever become white

Can one erase the other

Will God help us?

Why is black black and why is white white

Think about it

ABSOLUTE CONCENTRATION

What if God was one of us

How can you attest to that

Live your life according to the rules

So long you don't steal or kill that's the key to peaceful living

Intellectuals are your friends living single is never your wish

Until I find you my heart will continue to search for you

Love your life and live it to the fullest with me in your future

Attempt to harm nor tempt no one

Remember what you see is what you will get

Love is not a game I'm only being real

This is how it goes so be ready

Love will bring you and I together forever. Peace

CRUSH LOVE

She is an African diva unlike no other.

The thought of seeing you is joy.

I know you don't know me but this love is real.

That's why I took the time to pray for you each morning that you may come to me this night.

Know this self actualization is key to successful relationships.

Loving you is never a mistake and you are the kind every man should keep.

This is wisdom from me to you.

Even if I don't marry you I want you to be happy

Because this life is all you have,

So keep it strictly intellectual because you are an aristocrat.

You are a person of high intellect use it to your advantage because an unused mind is a terrible loss.

Please never deceive yourself because you are a lovable lady that's why I'm in love with you.

THE PURPLE DRESS

This purple dress reveals your physique

With the body of a goddess you are prettier than any super model
    alive

Your eyes shines brighter than they look

Your lips are more sensual than I can describe not detailing them is
    a loss

Kissing you make my heart want to tangle as it giggles

Your intelligence supports your beauty

Please remember loves stems from the heart not the mind

Although they say a mind is terrible loss if it is unused

Your destiny will always test your strength

Be ready to climb that hard rocky road

With that purple dress destination destiny is an easy thing

THE WHITE DRESS

She has a heart full of warmth

Your voice is filled with peace and joy

Your essence complete me

Thinking of you makes me feel satisfied even before any meal

Your presence I desire that my soul may find rest inside

I am sorry I turn my back on you

His Grace brought me back to you

I realize your life is worth more so I promised to cherish you and
never to abandon you.

Please remember God is real and marriage is His institution

Take heart that you and I may enter his court on that day.
Congratulations

Temptations

Temptations are not your portions

Though trials and tribulations tried to take your essence

But my strength destroyed your temptations

So from me to you God lives and He's alive

Fighting temptations are never easy but determination

Will always help you to succeed

Remember that and you will overcome

So you should have no worries regardless because my spirit dwells
within you.

Others doubted your existence and some discredited your existence
on earth

THIS RED ROSE

Mrs Omosa this red rose is for you

On this wedding day please remember you are the celebrant

A day like this come once in a life time

I'm glad I can be a part of you

My heart promise to love and cherish you with all it's got

The goal is to make you comfortable and be treated as the queen of
life

I know training your children will not be an issue because your parents have done a wonderful job raising you.

Your cooking speak of your home training

You have become my goddess for this and many reasons.

MARRY ME

Engagement is what I want

Without you the future is uncertain

You are my backbone and the confidence I stand upon

Making decisions become easy with you involved

Incredible achiever is what I have found in your spirit

You are a powerful force and a wife to be cherished

You are an unbreakable tool with the force of a storm

You are an indescribable human being welcome to my life

As your king I won't let you suffer.

I will be your shield against all odds.

Together we can set the foundation of our lives

You are the companion I have been looking for

Bonnie and Clide will never be close to who we are

Marry me so we can honeymoon in Tahiti

It's a place full of peace and joy better than oasis

You are an African queen ready for marital bliss

HER LIFE IS BRILLIANT

Your life is brilliant and you are beautiful

You will always be my wife

Your life is brilliant and you are an icon to be model after

A mother to two nations that's why you are Mrs. America

Your life is brilliant because you are a living testimony to all of us.

Your life is brilliant and fill with excellent zeal.

Your life is brilliant because you have an unquenchable love.

Your life is brilliant that's why you will be cherished forever

Your life is brilliant for your work will speak of it's creator

Your life is brilliant because you are the most beautiful young woman
living for today

Your life is brilliant because as an educator you help others to correct
their past that they may understand their present in order to
avoid future mistakes.

Your life is brilliant because you loved yourself first, and then your
children always

Your life is brilliant because you became a beautiful mother to all of us

Your life is brilliant and you will become a statue to be idolized

Her life is brilliant and beautiful for you will be a mother to be remembered from this day throughout all generations

My wife is brilliant and beautiful

I love you.

Ms. Keys

Your voice is one of a kind compare to no other

When you sing it's automatically known that you are on air

You have the most melodious tone I have never heard before

You are in your own class higher than your counter parts

You are a force in the industry an Icon to be model after

Idolizing you will never be a mistake

You have become your own signature from your head to your toes

Your record is a classic listening to your music soothes my soul

The goal is to meet you in person with hopes to see you sing live

You have been decorated with love and honor

Please hold your head up high.

PICTURE

Your picture is beautiful

it displays your essence and radiates your inner thoughts

your eyes are sharper than eagles eyes

your facial expression reveals your kindness

whatever you do don't lose your innocence

You are the most precious person unlike no other person I have seen

keep your head up and never be discouraged

life is full of ups and downs remember it

use your knowledge always and apply yourself

appropriately with wisdom then you will come out on top

above your counter parts

Imafidon's are brilliant seeds ask your father

study hard to show yourself approved.

There is success in our blood please don't contaminate it

Ms Vernon

She is an unknown soul recognized by me

Thought you could hide forever but you revealed yourself to me

Whether you hide or not darkness cannot comprehend your presence

Love yourself for you are my princess

So delicate and elegant you shine brighter than the sun

Your mind is full of knowledge so use it appropriately

That's the secret to Godly wisdom.

A most beautiful princess to a humble father is who you are.

Ms. Arie

She is an elegant lady full of grace empowered by God to persevere

Your vein is full of strength. You are brilliantly laced

Eternity should be your desired goal as a person.

You are an aristocratic icon.

Your smile could kill and your look's speak even louder words.

Love yourself it will keep you on top forever.

Remember one thing dignity is worth more than child's play. Peace.

Obama is NEXT! 4:58pm

Mr America both black and white

Full of grace empowered by God

 He is half man half amazing

chosen by God to lead

elect him and he will change your world

Obama is next it's time for a change

Trust him he won't let you down

Obama is next speaking boldly

ferociously capable never disastrous

Mr Intellectual if you are not sure ask (Harvard)

Obama is next is a prophecy from 2008..

BOSTON

Love it or hate it beantown is where I'm from

believe me or don't bean town is my home

Mandela is where I lay my head to rest

you can ask for me at carter's playground ballin

If you know Mandela check the apartments is all love never hating

receive me or not Boston is where i'm from

I have eyes like angels that;s why you can't miss me

always ballin at Bills Bar every Thursday

Love or hate us is time to put Boston on the globe, it's international

referring to my peeps, you can take it from here my job is done

all y'al from Boston it's your turn to shine.

PAIN

ReKonstruction

If you stand then stand remember your life is your aim because it should be your gain.

In the end you have yourself to blame not me.

Say it now so you won't have to say it again because Perfection is my aim and you can't follow me. Search for me if you want you won't find me

I am hidden like stealth in your heart from the very beginning and you didn't even know it.

God is great my eyes are open I'm only looking for love

I know enemies of my enemies don't want me to prosper discomfiting is what I have become thank God as from today I'm free from illness because he has blessed me with you as my bride from the spiritual to the physical.

Unknown

Mr and Mrs Charity giving is their aim

peace is their blessing and joy is their heart

entwined by God to give a million a year to a global cause for children and

another 1 million annually to Doctors without borders.

Stay blessed you are a force with global recognition

Mr. and Mrs Charity my goodwill ambassadors-remain blessed

Trust

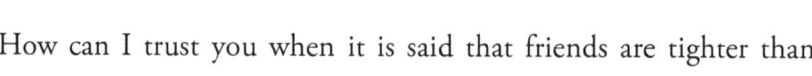

How can I trust you when it is said that friends are tighter than
brothers

When your number one enemy stem from your father's house

Oh well we will see who will last whether Judas or Joseph

I now realize this back stabber's are real

Is one thing to hear a tale from a dog's mouth, it's another to feel it
physically

Life is life right? I'm asking you the reader. How can you trust some
one who has hurt you one too many times. I have to be dead
right?

Oh we will see at the cross road.

SHAME

A stranger from an unknown location

She was sent by God to serve as my angel

She bought my groceries and Market Basket was the place

Though I don't know you but know this your heart was real

I wanted to ask for that number unfortunately shame struck because
you saved me.

I promise you this my eyes will find you to thank you in a special
way

It must happened because I trust my eyes because they were anointed
with salve

You know what they say only pure hearts can see God, that's why
you are my beatitude.

FOOT WEAR

He walk like a mean machine
Oh what an ugly looking being you are
Killing your brother's from the east was not enough
But you had to erased the one's from west too.
What a life you are living I hope you are not waiting to exhale
It might never come because we are all smokes.
Advice don't smoke your brain out.

SAY IT

You scratch my back then I will tell you how it feels

We must educate the children appropriately so they can learn how
to implement ideas

The currency is enough to be spread around

Instruction is okay but without power to get wealth

What are you being instructed for?

Other's have ideas but are unable to implement

I ask you how can you have an Mba and are unable to start your
own business

Let's think about it?

Cough drop flat

You wonder why you drop when you cough

Your system must be unclean

Check your brain stem because they are fill with dark chemicals

Listen to your heart so you won't pass out next time

If you do she won't be there this time.

I'm sure you know they never stay, it's in her nature not to.

Peace to you and not perfect peace maybe with caution you might
make it to the Grammy's.

Silent tears what a feeling

Ever so faithful

Redeemer is your master key

Her soul is real and your heart is sacred

you have never hated a soul but always full of love.

In college when I first met her

Child's play blinded me but I'm grateful she came back

After some years God reunited us

From now on togetherness is my aim

Never will I hurt you,

I promise I will always love you

I want you to know those lonely night are gone because your love
is real

The Lord lift up his countenance upon you and give you peace

STARDOM

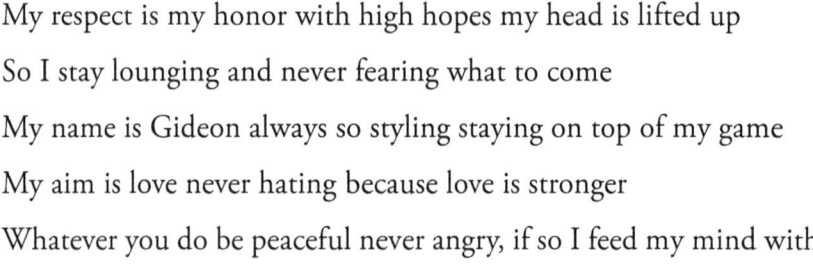

My respect is my honor with high hopes my head is lifted up

So I stay lounging and never fearing what to come

My name is Gideon always so styling staying on top of my game

My aim is love never hating because love is stronger

Whatever you do be peaceful never angry, if so I feed my mind with
wisdom

So I excel faster than my counter parts that's the trick.

Show Mercy

Mercy is her name ever so quiet with the force of a storm

whatever you do stay alive because it's not easy.

Most of all love yourself that is all and with determination aim high

so you can implement your ideas

And let God raise you beyond your imaginations.

Please follow your heart and ignore discouraging friends

above all continue to stand with all hearts.

DON'T GIVE UP

I tried so many times it never worked

I read and read but my brain could not understand

Even though my heart want me to know more

In 3 days I read "Makes Me Wanna Holla"

That's when my eyes were open

I was empowered with an amazing motivation that took me through
High school

Scholarships upon scholarship were presented to me but my brain
detained

My prosperity until now. So if you read without understanding just
pray

It will come.

GIDEON

A man of full of pain, filled with sorrow

He was constantly accompanied and clothed with silent tears at
night

Loneliness never left him until now because everything he tried
yielded failure

Adonai appeared to him one night and minister to him

Son your time is now believe with your heart and strenghten yourself

Though you are from the weakest tribe

I promise you this night you are different being because

"I have dedicated you a god, to prosper with an amazing anointing
because you were always obedience to your father's call"

Words not stones

Words are more powerful than stones

Physical wounds heal in time but words expressed inappriotely could kill

If care is not taken.

That's why is not adviseable to curse because if you have been anointed

By God then he has ordain you with tremendous power ask any minister they should know.

No more tears after this!

Excite me and see if I will laugh

Some are serious and others are not

But remember if I try and it didn't work

Don't give up because in the end when your time come

It will be automatic and your cheeks will smile even when you don't

want to

ZIKLAG

A place full of common people and peasants

Led by the one and only man who was an outcast

He was blessed with soldiers who were obedient and loyal

Both the old and the young followed him because he was highly
gifted with words of wisdom. Together they persevere

When one was hurt the others felt his pain

Spoil of war was what they placed their daily survival on

When his family was taken from him and his men

Some turn their back on him and threatened him.

But when the anointing came upon him he recovered everything.

ANNOINTING

Anointing is a teacher, it can command you

It can direct you by voice to wherever the sovereign Lord send you

If God says you will be this and that it will happen

Everyone on this planet earth is controlled by God even Christians.

Anointing can't lie or deceive you if you know him, he will help you

He's a deity check in first John 5.

Just as he has taught me he will teach you ask David

He will tell you what happened in Ziklag.

EDUCATE YOURSELF

Educate yourself my love so you can stand tall among the crowd

They say two is a couple and three is a company

Well this is from me to you an advice

One alone with education is stronger than two uneducated.

Set yourself apart because you have what it takes to reach where your
Destiny resides

For many are educated unfortunately few becomes successful

Remember you are educated please he who called you will surely see
you through,

I see you at the top already

your destiny is a beautiful picture at the mountain top.

So climb higher differentiation is your promoter never a quitter
because I know your spirit is full of zeal and strength.

What a beautiful hard worker ever so ready for life.

It's baggage cannot stop you so keep flying.

Remember in the end education will lift you up faster than your counter part.

minister joy and faithfulness will console you so long you don't lose your confidence.

PAIN

What is pain? Can it be described when it's upon you

Other's feel differently than you can but what about me

And you?

How do you feel it.

They say the strong will survive in the end

I tell you is not always the case because I learned something during
my ordeal

Death is stronger than life because you live for a while but death is
eternal

That's what pain can bring, eternity in a casket.

DEDICATED A GOD

Dedicated to idols

He clothed me with poverty

As a farmer it didn't work so I became poorer

I tried to educate myself it was not easy until now

epilepsy and his cousin seizure discomfited me

Wisdom led me to Christ for healing

Anointing took me through the Bible for 365 days and then some

Serious understanding shielded me and wisdom told me God has given me power to get wealth.

That's my goal so long I don't steal or kill it shall be done.

Silent Tears Amid thoughts

Life is what you make of it, if you like say it, its up to you nothing is like a bed full of roses for most. Others can see from afar what you can feel in your heart, that's just the way it goes nothing will never be the same stay in your relm unless you can maneuver the tough terrain call life semper fidelis. Get yours when the door is open or else it will close in your face just like that. Oh well don't say you were not warned. I washed my hands from your demise, good bye, I'm out

DEADBEAT FATHER

His name was Iyobo and it means help, we needed his presence and
companionship but he never stayed so he deserted his children

An Imposter that's who you are Mr Aibanye

so long I don't steal or kill I am going to express my feelings it's my
freedom and its constitutional

it's alright because this is my breakthrough

You left me to suffer for almost three decades

I've sewn my seeds Jesus has insured it

this is my time.

If you are wise ask Jesus for repentance

He'll will put a new and right spirit within you

ask David Solomon's dad because he stayed and took care of his.

That's where I will be different in my time

Procreation was never my wish lust was your food

advice don't be a snake repent because there's a curse on you

It is written do not provoke your children to anger ask Ephesians,
and David he will tell you from Kings.

Educate yourself because

I'm not your enemy I am just expressing myself I never asked for
this.

Be a man like your father

He was a real father and I am his Incarnation

Single mothers no more

Ms Simone please stay home tonight Damien will provide Oh I'm sorry I forgot you have a dozen of us kids Oh well we have to eat since dad decided to become a player I tell you he's cursed. single mother's is what we don't need because education is key. Perfection should be our aim. I hate men that abandon their wives with children. How can they survive during procreation did infants asked to be born? Repentance is what dead beat fathers need to do. If it was up to me I will make them pay but I will live that up to God to judge. Society should be at peace but it is not because there is violence everywhere. In my heart when my time come I will take care of mine

BACKBONES

She was single and deserted but together they are my inspiration. The sources of my strength, through the dark nights their presence kept me alive. Through numerous tribulations and trials when friends deserted me their spirits encouraged me, so I kept trekking until now. So I'm grateful with a humble heart I boldly pay tribute to the dead and the living. Thank God I came through their blood line, it's a tale to be told including the endless nights of story-telling never left my memory. It was like yesterday in Oka village back in 1989

when I saw the dead for the first time my heart left me without feelings and I became numb and almost dumb. That is when I knew this life is all we've got.

Thank you for not leaving when I needed you.

One passed and one stayed. Rest in peace Mrs Imafidon.

May God keep you and bless Mrs. Ijesuorobo.

A custodian full of grace with amazing heart to love black or white

The day you read this you will see me in your dream ask Eliphaz it's in Job.

This is my relief whether you hate me or love me it's a rap. I'm just a voice

God bless you Mr. Aibanye be a man if you love your mother you should love me too

you you deserted her so you know you killed her. I thank God I buried her for you and your brother as a child back

1989, read my backbones she will tell you herself. You never called never cared ask her spirit. If you like tell Shrilanka to curse me it's reversed.

EPILEPSY

Epilepsy is a disease of the brain it turns humans into vegetables unable to focus and cannot implement ideas. Unless you know Christ you will suffer knowing him is peace because he died for you and he went from rich to grass for you. Epilepsy stole his destiny, his dreams to (become....). but Christ came to restore and slapped Epilepsy and his agents you know him (Satan). Where he's from the east where stars stay shining but because they saw his future as they flew into him during their rituals they met his angel and evaporation occurred. Epilepsy and his cousin were eliminated you know him they call him seizure.

BIBLE

Basic is what I am just like barney kiss me to understand me because my breath will correct you

Instructor was what I was and still is, from E1 to E4 I was instructed so I became a corrector

Before leaving you know the Corps It wasn't easy but I had to, you know find my own academically, so civilian or not a civilian once a marine will always be a marine, oorah.

Leaving is what I do often, it has become the anxiety in me and I need an ante dote. maybe a 50 cal. can or a saw to clean my system, you know just like the valley flowing peacefully

Earth is full of greener pasteurs only wise ones can tread and graize it, you know them 3 percenter's, whatever you do remember the children must eat beacause it's all about the greens.

THE GOD'S LIVES-IT'S THE REVERSE

The call 'em devil dogs aka gods lives it's the reverse

the highest fraternal order on earth,

the toughest groups of brethren

full of diversity, their missions are incredible

the fewest and the proudest the marines always surviving difficult

terrains, trial is our gain and tribulation is our blessing

I know because I was there for eight years

They make men out boys, it was a blessing to serve with the breth-

ren. Thank you Mr. Commandant, God bless the UNITED

STATES MARINES

Stay alive, semper fi.

JEBROSOTO IT'S SPIRITUAL

I am what I am what you feel is what will eventually manifest if it's to better the society then its all-right with holy spirit, u know where the spirit of God dwells there is liberty, so if freedom it's scriptural get it. If the son set you free it's a rap. Christ is all there is for most-in the end who is Lord of all Satan or Jesus-if u don't get it study to show thyself approved because it's scriptural that's the wisdom of Moses the general who became the high priest who saved you by putting the snake on the cross to destroy the lustful desire in your heart. Love me or hate me I will still die for you that's what Jesus said. No man can never do that maybe if you die for your country as a soldier, a seaman, an airmen, or a marine that's what real men do. What am saying is unless you served don't disrespect the military love them. You enjoy your sleep because of them, and if I were you I buy them a beer or two during liberty to set their heart at peace- Now that's **GOSPEL**.

INTERNATIONAL RELATIONS

Nigeria a place like no other

Different from every other African country

Full of intellectuals always on their knees

Praying at the mountains in communications

With God ask Bishop David Oyedepo better yet check him at

Faith Chapel Church. Yep that's right

Anointing is his strength a man with amazing heart filled

With Grace and faith laced with immeasurable wisdom sent by God
    to set the youth free

A man of high intellect if you are unsure ask Covenant University.

A Soldier's Fear

Just about the fourth watch

While on fire watch with private hotel

Lightning struck our base

Out of fear my knees began to shake and I began to quiver

Enemy on site cried out my mouth

It was a straight bullet along with its cousin mack-19

That struck our central command

Before you know it General Thompson 's tent exploded

Sgt Holmes quickly gathered the squad together

We returned fire back to the enemy direction

Minutes later they were doomed.

What you should know

You rise in the east and eat in the west. If you feel it do it like the marines always taking actions unless you experience it, it never occurred. Feelings are significant it will direct your path if you have what it takes to hear it.

BEING REAL

I say it as I hear it, boldness is what I am. If you steal it it's alright, I will tell you that it takes two not one because one will suffer but when they are enjoined fame is acclaimed. If that's how it goes then don't stain your blood because it will cause your seeds to suffer, I'm talking about your descendants.

Then its a curse but not on I because I'm skipping it like king David you know him Solomon's dad.

Unfailing hands

On your own this time it might happened

After much trial and tears shed all you need now is to believe with
your heart

With those unfailing hands and never looking backward achieve-
ment is in your corner right ahead smiling at your shadow.

The thought of raising those hands to work brings happiness to your
heart

Curse is one with lazy hands and that cannot be your portion

The essence and spirit of hard work lies in your hands and without
them life will be unbearable.

Waking up each morning depends on your hands please hold on to
those unfailing hands

Dear friend

Your heart is purer than you think, in essence stay undefiled

Precious is what you were named please remain special and you have become closer to me than most friends will ever be.

Your look is sweet and precious when you dress you can make a man's eyes like pop eye's the sailor. pop

I thank God you were sent at the right time.

Your friendship is warmer than the summer heat

Please remember you are an intelligent queen and it will take you places.

I promise to love you with more intensity that you gave.

You will never be empty and loneliness will never be your friend.

Because you gave yourself to my service, I will remain humbly grateful.

Thanks to a dear and special friend.

THINK ABOUT IT

Without work will a man be able to survive

If I decide to stop working today

What will I eat tomorrow

What about the children

Who will feed them and who should be responsible

Why is nurturing important

 Does it hold a place in our society

I'm asking you the reader

Will you say something

JUST REALIZE

I just realize why I never have to wonder since I am blessed with
    numerous wisdom above Solomon's, yet nothing has materialized
Is it me or is it wisdom
Things should be easier because I'm blessed with wisdom right
But what will feed me if there is no manifestation
Can wisdom feed me or can God
I need to know?

LIFE VERSUS TIME

Are life and time on the same wavelength

Will one be above the other?

Why is it that in this global village when others rise the others are
    going to sleep

Will you ever realize what your future entails

Are your eyes open enough to feel the race of life versus time

Who will win

You were 2 few days ago and today you have climbed against the
    ladder to 85

Suddenly death is at the door knocking to enter

Perhaps you should reconsider your options before it's tool late

I just realize time and life will never run on the same track.

THE HUNGRY AND LONELY VETERAN

I am blind and crippled

After returning home from defending my country failing health
struck me

So I ask who can help me

Will the Government or will the Veterans Administration

So I have become a begger on the streets

Who will compensate me for my loss

Will God or the Government

What is the essence of fighting to defend you if this is the reward

Remember all veterans not just on veterans day

Companionship counts more than words

Visit them as you read this expression.

MORNING STAR EQUAL MAN IN THE WILDERNESS

A man of courage and honor, often lost in thoughts

He was found guilty on several occasions but the morning star became his companion

Each time he was accused it became a blessing

When they were asked to chose who to set free between him and another who was worthless.

They blindly chose the thief to stay and him to die

Who knows maybe if the thief was killed, there would be no stealing today

Let's think about for a moment.

UNITED STATES

Undivided attention should be our aim as a country

Not inviting envy along with racism we can fix past mistakes

Initial mistakes should be forgiven and forgotten if you believe God lives

Togetherness is sweeter if we understand one another with mutual respect irregards of status in society

Equality is the only answer that's why it was written in the constitution, advice let's respect the constitution

Division should not be our portion as a country let alone hatred

Sisterhood is an example of what this country need, absolute love

Talking is never enough action is better spoken when it is carried out

Act now before it's too late, be proud to speak your mind and most of all love your country

Teamwork is how the early father's overcame struggles and inequality beyond that God stayed by their side.

Everyone should be ready for love because it is the only answer to peace and unity

Survival will cause only the determined to arrive at the top.

REVIVED

Set free to prosper

He had no desire to lust after mundane things

So focus was a tool in his right hand

With concentration he became an achiever

He had no competition, what he want is what he got

With a new heart and mind he became a different being

Full of love instead of lust

Lost souls

At 15 some run away from home because of unsettled issues between
families

Some end up doing drugs, others enter to prostitution in haste to
become independent

I ask you, is it worth it? Will running away solve the problem.

Maybe we should ask the parents too, why and how come?

What happened to them, I mean if a child is raised appropriately
things would have been different.

If you ask me there should be no reason for single mothers or single
fathers

Who will save them now, we all know life on the street is not safe.

In the end love should bring them home.

CONFESSIONS

Confess your love to one another and be reunited

Love yourself and your wife

Remember the wilderness was a place where the two of you survived

If you remember all the rough roads she followed you through she
should be first always

Remember the children because they count too

Nine months she carried them for you that's why mother's day
should be special

At 5 in the morning they rise to do it all over but first they feed the
children

Father's count too without their presence there would be no male
figure to be idolized.

After much work they should return home.

SOUL TRAIN

An unstoppable icon was what you became

Lust ruled your heart until now but love took over in the end

Enjoy your life and live it to the fullest death and loneliness should
   not be a constant companion

If you believe you can be saved

Exchanged is what the result yielded in the end.

Muzik

It will revive your soul, is a place where I cannot be disturbed

It clean loneliness and evaporates depressions

What an eye opener, it is the greatest awakening and ministry

It is more important than food because in it you will find the healing formula

Let them rap, let them sing

Watch them and see if violence is not erased completely

Muzik in the end is an ante dote that serve as a solution to violence

Ask your larynx he will tell you that your mind enjoys it too

Even their eyes along with their facial expression changed too

It is a sign of repentance that's how you pay your price to society

RESPECT

Wives respect your husbands

Single life is loneliness because friends smile with you when things
 are good

But your husband will always be there even when things are bad

That's what it means to cleave to one another. If you are wise let
 your husbands be first.

Every decision should be his in the end after much family discussion

Whether the woman is wealthier than the man should not count.

So remember friends come and go.

THOSE LEGS

They are insured by God not money

Love what He gave you because the beginning is better than the present

Use your resources wisely above all trust yourself

Family is much more important than friends

Give them the right mentality maybe you don't know you are supposed to be an Idol.

Pain is remembrance

Remember who you used to be

Because the beginning is always better for all us

After much oppression some cannot revive

But the solution is revival and nothing else

That is why pain cannot be your companion

You have what it takes to get up

Reconstruction is what your end will be.

ANTE DOTE

Is the greatest medicine on earth

It heals and reverse curses

The ancient time can tell why

Even native americans knows

It cannot divide but it will bring unity

Try it and see if it will not set you free

Not even a snake can survive without it

Freedom is what it brings to all of us.

CONSOLIDATION

Reconsider forgiveness as a nation it is possible

Just look at yourself and realize how much you have changed

The beginning is better please remember old time friends

Some were closer than him, they are the reason you should come
out of the closet

You have become a cat, wilderness cannot contain you

You were born to be a star remember you are highly acclaim by your
people

Reunion

A child at heart is what he still is

But with determination he brought them together

They shared laughter and smiled together as they ate

Dancing was next, it brought them joy

Their soul rejoiced because they became one

Grandma and grandpa remembered how far they've come

Cousins, nieces, nephews, uncles, and aunts enjoyed each other's company

With one heart and mind they seized the moment

While reminiscing to take a look at the past procreations

The moon and the sun laughed at them with much gratification.

REPROBATE MIND

They thought they were from the east but they were fooled because
    they came from the north

Wisdom did not save them.

They gathered themselves together to plot evil

Their resources evaporated and they were depleted

They tried over and over it did not work

What is wisdom if there is no obedience to the greatest deity

Who created the heavens

Medicine could not solve the situation any more

Confusion led them to no avail

Those they hate became who they idolized in the end.

BLACK PLANET

Is who I am

A place where my mind find peace

Different from face book and you cannot compare it to myspace

It is full of love with words exchanged friends will know you are real

Are you worth dying for?

If you resist yourself you will lose your concentration

Step up to him say it they way you feel it

Whether they laugh at you or not you will still be idolized

Forgiveness cannot repeat itself because perfection should be your
goal

Love yourself because you are highly respected by them

You are definitely worth loving talk less of dying for

I'M A VOICE

Anointed by twelve prophets in the end I became a priest

Living single was my training till my graduation

It was known as a right of passage, after much which sin couldn't hold me down

The voice that is real is what I have, blessed by God himself to prosper

If you need understanding ask Moses he lives in exodus

By voice I anointed you that's why you will see me in your dreams tonight

It's not my fault it happened this way but remember this in time of need just remember God lives. Peace be with you!

Unsettled hearts

Remember who you were before you left

As always the beginning is better than presently

All you need is to fine tune your voice, then the industry is yours
for the taken

He was loved and respected by most.

He was more than a man, you became a voice adored by many

I'm glad you came back to your senses and you came out of the
closet

Welcome home cousin, remember this time to stay till the end.

SHED SO MANY TEARS

Past and present kept me alive my enemies couldn't take me

In time of need God sent His Angels to deliver me from their storms

I couldn't sleep at times at night because of restlessness and demons
trying to take my life

But in the end like Solomon wisdom led me to overcome because
I was empowered by Gideons anointing. Though I was weak I
became strong with just three hundreds men the opposition was
defeated.

I AIN'T MAD AT YOU

Street life didn't help me either, upon graduating high school

Thoughts of dropping out of college plagued me

God told me to grab my basketball to go to the basketball court to calm mind down

While others took on drugs, hey remember whatever they do have consequences

Advice street life won't always help because the past will follow you if you need understanding ask your descendants or better yet check the progress of your ancestors because they ended up the same way you will if you don't change.

So get your mind right. If you need a peace of mind go to church.

REVERSE IT

How can the junior become the leader of a nation

Can you skip the elder and bypass the rest

It's not possible unless you are David who after much work in God's
court yard was crown king and leader of the world.

Whether you are a jew, greek, black, white, Hispanic, Native
American, and Syrians

In the end we are all one flesh and one heart so reverse it.

THE PROMISE

His promise was his backbone never to be broken by him or you

He was sent to be your senator and you are supposed to be his constituents

16 years in the senate he came to no avail, it's time for you to come home

We want to hear what is so special about what you did in Washington

Mr celebrity the senate is not a place for you to fall asleep

It's time for a change I promise you that!

Mr. Senator

Repent and follow your wife

You should love your children, your heart lies in the hand of your
first girlfriend

Whom you dumped in high school

Stealing is not a game because she will ask you

So you know it's vice versa

Ask her children because they all look like you even though you
didn't father them

It's a mystery taught me by God, if you see me ask so I can direct
you to revelation.

HEART BEAT OF AMERICA

He was known as the land of culture and tradition

Unfortunately those who stood up for him to rule were blind

Today there is nothing to show for eight years and he left the children, college students, and the elders broke.

Embezzlement became your food, eat until you can't eat no more

I promise you there is a day of reckoning and it's around the corner.

Paradise or not stand

Standing always will cause you to be seen but with boldness it's a rap

You will go beyond recognition, they will fall for you

Then you will have no choice unless you hide for a while like
Howard Hughes

Then you must chose the best out of the bunch

Sisters or not be ready for the taken.

He loves women that love to dress and show it off like they mean it.

THE SPIRIT OF AMERICA

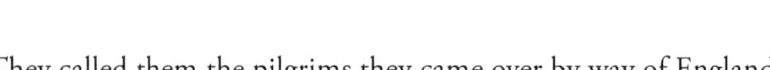

They called them the pilgrims they came over by way of England

If you ask me what about the Native Americans.

Who is the real spirit of America?

Let's think about it. I'm just a voice sent to judge your conscience

Humans are humans in the latter let's remember they count too.

106 & Park

Oh oh 106 & park is the place to be.

A place that got black to be uglier than ever.

The darker the berry Tupac said the sweeter the juice,

Jay-z say's it's me and my girl friend,

Nastradamus is an African king,

player please I'm only here to promote "Love Expressions" think about it, the album is next followed by the movie,

Nas can play my older brother.

My mind is in the hands of God and He said to you to check John 3:8.

Tell Denzel to holla at me I got movie ideas I want to sell to him.

Each poem is a movie that is what 106 & Park stands for "Love Expressions"

God Bless you and keep you.

ONE-UNITED

They were known as unity, they formed a bond stronger than cheese
cake

Until Uncle black sold them out

Oh well in 5 years guaranteed they will head into a recession

Uncle Genius came to their rescue

That's what happened when they make it in the hood and instead
of staying to fix it

They bounce. I wonder why? Why do you think that is so?

It's a shame all of our role models packed out of the hood to hide in
the suburbs.

It remind of Adam and Eve.

SHOW MERCY

Mercy is her name ever so quiet with the force of a storm

whatever you do stay alive because it's not easy.

Most of all love yourself that is all

Be determine so you can aim high, then you can implement your
ideas

And let God raise you beyond your imaginations.

Please follow your heart and ignore discouraging friends

Remember love knows no boundries

Study to show yourself approved Ms Egharevba

You are my idol and never to be mistaken

If loving you is not in my heart I wouldn't write to you.

above all continue to stand with all hearts.

MTV

Museek Television is where I want to get married.

I would keep it real if it was up to me.

I would ask God to get me M. TV's greatest veejay's Mr Carson daly and my brother Sway.

I need Carlson sex appeal to move the crowed and Sway's vernum to diffuse the air waves into the the radio station nationwide.

Help me God I want your amazing Grace backing me up.

Since Christ was my brother give me his authority from gethsemane.

Apostle Peter please tell Christ to heal my soul with Diddy's vernum and LL Cool J's anointing to acquire female status to back me up in my lolo.

God bless you and keep you.

So God reincarnated me and I became Lazarus

Raised on the 3rd day Jesus did it's in John

IDOLIZING EDOSA

Idolizing Edosa was never a mistake

You have the heart of a god

Raised by America born in Nigeria

Boston beats limo is coming back

If God exist we will do it again

Thank you for doing more than Iyobo it means help

I promise I will pay you back in time

I remember how you took us on vacations to Disney world and
   beyond

How the road trip was worth it all. you drove to Vermont irregards
   of the weather with determination you brought me here.

1994 was the year I touch down at logan

We were the seeds of another and you came without prejudice and
   took over as a dad

Eramwen Ne Edosa it's your time to shine. Uwuese it means thanks.

Please remember this, if God exist destiny will not deny you,

Heaven has a crown waiting for you

The greatest thing a son could experience is to eat from the same
plate with a man like you

Once again Uwuese it means thanks.

Death try to take me and you rallied around for me

HEAVENS GREATEST DAUGHTER

If I were to come back again

I would ask God to put you in my family

Being around you has been a blessing

Your presence and your cooking I cannot deny

I admit your love is real sis

Keep up the good work

Your reward is in the hand of God

And it's coming, God loves you EHI OWENS

Most of all Wizdom Loves you.

CHRISTIAN

Mayhem is a Christian from Rhode Island

A brother to Wizdom, your voice on the airwaves sweetens my soul

Keep it up, destiny cannot deny her children

It's in your blood Imafidon's are brilliant seeds

Rip it Mayhem I can feel your vernum spitting verbs plus nouns without simily.

Our heart one destiny Mayhem

Your life is in God's hand now, remember he loves you

He gave Holy Spirit to guide you

From this day on I command generational sin out of lives

Love will take us home from here on

God bless you and keep you

God make his face shine upon you and lift up his countenance on you

God bless you and give you peace as you tread the waters of life.

Love from your only brother.

EDO BROADCASTING SERVICE

Ebs was my idol

Growing up to watch late night shows it was real

So my heart still yearn for you, even after trekking to U.S.

Keep up the stylistic and investigative work you do

Always so thorough and live, you are always on air

Stay alive ebs, it's your turn to shine

My Greatest Gift

Mary Owens, you are my backbone

Denying your existence would make me a lier

9 months I spent in your belly was not a joke

The day I came out you and I began our greatest journey and we
are still on it

I thank God for Edosa Owens and you.

Don't worry we were born to prosper, God promised me this.

In Deuteronomy he reminded me that he has given me power to
get wealth

As long as I remain obedient to his call, his anointing will teach me
Your suffering days are over Mary Owens.

Wizdom says thank you for being the world greatest mother. God
bless you Mary Owens

My heart loves you.

THE GREATEST KING

Mr. Ukuakpolokpolo the greatest King that God has ever anointed

I was born the year the king of Benin was crown

That's my wisdom back in 79,

He has the anointing of King David

A man highly anointed by God to lead his children (Iviedo)

He's a god with the boldness of his father

He was anointed to protect Edo State with his V

ernum Omonoba nerhamwen God Bless you sir.

INDEPENDENCE TELEVISION

Of course we all know what you stand for

Mr. Generation X, leading the way throughout Edo

Remind me of M-tv Africa

I-tv rocks you should rock the music scene in Benin too

The youths await your genesis it means the time is now.

Live on Independence Television.

I got your business anointing, it is ready for commencement.

OREDO LOCAL GOVERNMENT CHAIRMAN

Raising Edo is not an easy Job

If not God wouldn't have put you there

Continue to teach and train us Mr. Chairman

Your reward is in the hands of God.

Heaven awaits you and your crown is on the way

Because you love your duty

God said he will support you

Edo Children listen to your father and obey the rules

Rock on Mr. Chairman, may God grant you long life.

EDO STATE GOVERNOR

Thank you for what you are doing

It takes a man with high intellect to hold and manage a state like Edo

The bible says you must be able to run your household before running a city, then a state.

Your education with your status has proven that you are capable

Continue to hold your head up sir.

God keep you and bless you.

www.ingramcontent.com/pod-product-compliance
Lightning Source LLC
Chambersburg PA
CBHW051213120626
46547CB00013B/1331